UNDER THE CAPSIZED BOAT WE FLY

UNDER THE CAPSIZED BOAT WE FLY

NEW & SELECTED POEMS

GAIL WRONSKY

WHITE PINE PRESS / BUFFALO, NEW YORK

White Pine Press
P.O. Box 236
Buffalo, NY 14201
www.whitepine.org

Publication of this book was supported by public funds from the New York State Council on the Arts, with the support of Governor Andrew M. Cuomo and the New York State Legislature, a State Agency.

Cover Painting: Vasily Kandinsky, (1866–1944) *Small Worlds II (Kleine Welten II)* from *Small Worlds (Kleine Welten)*. 1922. Copyright © ARS, NY. Lithograph from a portfolio of twelve prints, six lithographs (including two transferred from woodcuts), four drypoints, and two woodcuts. Publisher: Propyläen-Verlag, Berlin. Printer: Reineck & Klein, Weimar. Edition: 230. Digital Image copyright © The Museum of Modern Art/Licensed by SCALA / Art Resource, New York.

Printed and bound in the United States of America.

ISBN 978-1-945680-45-8

Library of Congress Control Number: 2020930088

For Shark
For Marlena

" . . . we should keep on proposing Paradise, even if the evidence at hand might indicate that such a pursuit is folly."

— *Raúl Zurita,*
translated by Jack Schmitt

TABLE OF CONTENTS

New Poems

Under the Capsized Boat We Fly

Again the Gemini are in the Orchard

TWENTY-THREE

In the sweet time of my first age,
wishing to speak,
I confessed in the meadow
by a stone. I talked of everything:
how I loved him;
how my hair in the lamplight looked
red and surreal;
how I took pleasure in the distant
deaths; how I daily fled
the belling of my womb; continue
to love him; and my little speech
about the necessary emptiness;
(how murder is more meaningful
than other deaths); my vanity
about a certain orchid gown; god,
and how I drown in the orchid night
for love of him . . .

The she, the stone,
to her ghostly form quickly
returning, made me, alas,
an almost live and frightened woman.

(It was as if a swarm of
crystal insects,
trying somehow to speak,
got tangled
in a cloud of gauze.)

This is how I met her.
This is how I met my muse.

SHE AND I

(homage to Leonora Carrington)

I.
It's otherworldly, really,
how she comes and goes,
a winding and unwinding wisp,
a blue oval. Do you like
poetry? I ask her. *No.*

She cannot help it
that her lamentations aren't
always as melodious
as the other
seductive voices of the night.

Psychic waste—that
was our fate. A briefly
eternal psychosis for two.
Or was it otherwise?

II.
Born once in the palm
of mitten-shaped Michigan
out of Estrella by Jorge
or out of Matilda by Paul.
The litany of *madres lindas*
and *les noms des pères* is long.
Leonora was born many times
onto the earth's cold bosom.
Once as a horse
and she showed me,
throwing herself into snow.
When she got up
her whiteness was thunderous
like that of a waterfall—
her fine limbs
were like arrows and her mane
it was made of white plant roots
and floated around her wet face.

III.
Here's Leonora in a nutshell:

(Sometimes a picture covers more
than name or image.)

IV.
Leonora Borealis
a feline bride
woke up wanting more
found less
couldn't make the transition
and died.

To this day I remember her funeral cortège
with its four giant horses
marching slowly
its wheels like stiff explosions
turning slowly
her carriage a music box
the plink plink plink of the dirge

and the people weeping weeping
and the miserable priest saying
Here is the pale corpse of the frail Leonora
or Here is the small corpse of the tall . . .

I couldn't hear him
I could only read his red lips
through the transparent coins
through the transparent lid
through the translucent sky
bag of liquid
we broke with our heads.

V.
According to her, the best
root vegetable in Russia is
the beet. And
if she had it to do over again
she might. But sometimes,

when I'm settled
larva-like
in the fat of my primrose quilt,
a cool pillow over my head, I hear
the beatings she delivers
to herself:

the sounds of an animal
suffering unwillingly.

VI.
She loves a man:
Joseph Tragedy.

Not like Dachau
or Hiroshima,

it's inner misery
obsesses him.

She says that when
she kissed him

stars fell out
of his eyes, and the ground

burned them.
Why do you love him?

Because it's what I do—
I'm the moon over abstraction.

Why aren't you with him?
Not out of fear

and not indecision.
The mere weight of the body

won't permit it.
I am weary;

he is weary;
God is weary;

our hearts are so weary
they beat
every six hundred years.

VII.
When I asked her why she came to see me
she said, It's a semiotic
too complex for reasonography.

When I asked her if she liked this beach
she said, It's a semiotic too complex . . .

Her insight was unforgivable.

VIII.

At first when she leaves me I experience great
fits of laughter—a great disappointment to my
mother, who has her illusions about the family's
sanity. Then later I'm forced to wonder what
the significance is of a love not quite dead;
how am I to interpret the language of olive
trees; why does the gravedigger weep at the
sight of a bed? Because nothingness comes to no
good. Are you scared? Leonora would tell you
to put someone's hands on your head.

IX.
This is the parrot asleep in its cage.
This is the makeup disguising your age.
These are the letters that fall from your
pen. Leonora,
Leonora, Leonora, Leonora.

(The grand jilt of wings,
the lilacs, the cypress, your face,
Leonora)

A fullness too large to replace.

X.
Her instructions:

Turn off the radio.
(The clock takes over.)

Stifle the clock.
(There's no turning off time.
The flies take over.)

Kill the flies.
(It's the wind.)

Wind stops.
(Your own breath—
sigh after sigh—
all effort and repression.)

Hold your breath.

And remember
(she is now a raven,
flipping her black head coquettishly)

This
is your last day, but it is not
your very last day.

XI.
I want you to remember that I'm speaking
out of hard times now,
out of the hammer-down of year after year,
out of the land of diminishing choices,
the limited shape
of a life, a bit of trauma.

Doesn't it always come down to its tokens—
snatches of voice, the borrowed
jewelry of time,
the ghosts at the edge of the pond
throwing petals on water?

XII.
There are no lives left but
the ones after
which might or might not . . .

What I know of the twilight is nothing,

I walked to the west to get closer to truth
then so much was on fire
I could not begin to arrest it.

XIII.
The last time she came was in yellow October.
It was strange, a vaporous night.
(I say that, but the moon had risen
tough and clean above the vivid canyons.)

She woke me with cowbells
and spoke with her blue
xenon lips. What she said,
I wrote down.

When I woke again in the white
royalty of sunlight, I was happy.
Wasn't the sky lucid?
Weren't the bright leaves alive?

Then I read what I'd written—
elliptical rhymes about how time passes
then turns around and passes again
then repeats its past passings.

I lived out the rest of this life suicidal,
her luminous shadow
cerulean, perfumed,
in front of me and behind.

A Postscript

Years from now,
so little will be left to say.

So I'll say: *Everything*
is a euphemism for literal death.
Even this.

(I'll be sitting in my room
brushing away a few fruit flies—
my hair down or up.
I'll be wearing, oh,
an old striped dress . . .)

Look, she'll say, appearing
out of cloudy nowhere,
again the gemini are in the orchard.

Our trees, which have always been
paltry, will be
bowed with the weight
of incredible fruits.

So I'm writing, and rotting,
and waiting
for the ripening.

WEIRD BEACH

Salt Lake City

The newness is an eternity
of drive and the exotic.

And even as I let myself
pretend the exclusive beauty
of possibility away, it shows me
again that I can't—

no matter how painful or frightening
in this vast place it is
to have known union.

Do you feel the rhythm
that anchors my elements
in this storm of fear and stillness?

To be in your presence is beyond
imagination. I walk, I sit
silent in the offensively hot city.
I ride the stale winds of the bus.
I watch people, the traveling
crowd carrying on its flow—
a misguided tributary—wearing
pioneer white.

THE OTHER

If her heat persists
I'll rake and seed in here
and he'll come knocking.

She might be dead, he says,
although her heat persists—

so warm that
you could incubate an egg in her.
And he comes knocking—

the one whose smile
through the snowstorm's
like a white fish flipping up an avalanche.

And yet her heat persists.

Her eyeballs roll like onions in a pan.
The moths hang onto her bedclothes.

When he comes knocking
her hair reaches toward him.

To be alive is nothing
if her heat persists—
and if he comes knocking.

THE ULTIMATE UNKNOWABILITY OF WOMEN

for Karen

I.
You must understand there is no pleasure
like being in another woman's house,
sitting in her kitchen—her husband

asleep, a deep shape
breathing in a deeply tangled sea—
her children asleep, too,
mining dream's macadam . . .

II.
A woman has written a story
about the time her friend was pregnant
and she advised her to have the abortion.

In the story,
the narrator wants her friend to
have the child: *I want her to know*
what I know, she says.

There is something they both know
(to hide is to live?)

but neither one of them is speaking.

III.
The secret about Mary,
a woman I knew in Virginia,
is that she loved Bill more
than he her
even though everyone thought
it was the other way.
They're both dead now.

I'm trying to write a letter
to my lover: *My Beloved . . .*

What do you say?

I write with the milk from my breasts:
white ink on white paper.

Then of course you explain—
it's a joke. You were pulling
the wool on the page.

PARTING

My ugly new love
lost his first
wife in the bath-
tub now I'm
going blind I
can imagine only
the distances

An archangel
tickles my shoulder
with flame
In another few
years he will ask
for my phone number

Ask what you like
What I like is
simply the notion
of parting at death
of seeing in darkness
of wearing an
afterlife dress
and escaping forgiveness

I'll recover if
you point to me
forever and whisper
cadaver Of course
that's not vision

I lie like a sunbeam
amazed
at the edge of the page

THE MAIN ATTRACTION

Wordsworth's "Intimations" ode,
then, is not only a poem, but, among
other things a parable about poetry.
        — Cleanth Brooks

How now
come see the tiny cow
it's only two-and-a-half inches tall

used to be a professional pall-bearer
at the ant farm
then it lost that leg

come on and see it

it does a great imitation of Mae West
you know
swaying a little bit top heavy
why don't you come up and see it

I bet it could get a college degree
in being cute
and knowing what's what

Why just the other day
it looked at me like it know'd
what I said to Brenda last night
which was:

Quit crying bitch
that little cow
needs us to be brave

Ceci n'est pas un morçeau de fromage

There are objects that get by without names.
Why don't you seal some of this air
inside an empty aquarium
and call it *air*
or call it *Gail*
and leave the rest of me to wander
past the long dirty windows overlooking
the Garden of Eden Cafe and Knife Factory?

Let's lift the street and eat
the rutabagas underneath it.
Maybe we'll strike cheese
and call it happiness, or fall in love
and call it happiness.

A CURSE

As they walked through the field of discarded
refrigerators he thought, how strange
that these remain refrigerators, even though
at any moment, they could become trees.
She thought, the inventions of men
are inseparable from my oppression.

Suddenly they are dancing in a mirrored
        ballroom,
alone but reflected a thousand times,
and their eyes are blue and on fire
like the tiny continuous flames in the earth's
center incinerator. The moon
pours wine into a glass and places it beside
its black bed. A shooting star burns
to the ground in front of them,
leaving a crater full of emeralds. He says,

this is the place where once we picked
watercress. Soon we will be on the beach.

I would smile, says the woman, though by now
he is waltzing away from her, if I had teeth.

DYING FOR BEAUTY

I Died for Beauty

Día de los Muertos

What can be said
except—I want to lie with you
for a long time, skull-
to-skull, my sugar bridegroom.

Our hands are just bones now;
our jewelry has all dropped off!
And *mi ropa de novia*—
nothing but soured satin, brown-edged
lace. Our colonial aspirations!

Your grin is so fixed, *calavera.*
It is one of the things I admire
most about you
in my contemplating-eternity mode,
or when one bony finger (yours?
mine?) articulates a languid circle
in the shallows just below
my pelvic hollow.

from THE EARTH AS DESDEMONA

Othello: *I will kill thee / And love thee after.*

Unerringly,
let us talk of graves.

Tuesday, January 24:

to use language
to illuminate or
even to locate her

to speak of the body and of the earth
of copper, rivers

as if to describe them were

      *

to save anything.

Desdemona,

a lime-green hummingbird
suddenly busies herself
in the bare branches of a neighbor's
peach tree

where last autumn hundreds of heavy peaches
hung. But
today I prefer the spiked protestation of the yucca

its dozen raised fists fraught with blades

the dare it makes in the air above the backyard.

The few new leaves lifting
on the tips of the peach tree's diligent branches
convince me

of what? The accuracy and depth of this grief.

Wednesday.

Certain elements of the dream are open
to revision. But the body is always
dead.

Instincts, the psychic says,
tell me
the man had no pity.

(I feel sorry for his mother, said the mother
of the dead girl. To raise a child
that vicious and just not know.)

   *

Copper.
Archipelago.
Mother.
Revolution.
Silk ovals.

(Do we suggest the possibility of replacement—
copper for copper?)

Friday.

A few small leaves. A couple of biscuits stuffed with butter
and avocado honey. Southern Comfort. *Lime*-green
branches among the brown. Imagine an ice-stuck river,
after a cruel and thorough winter, shifting,
rushing beneath the surface, and finally, the disruption,
revolution, water going crazy with the strangeness
of its own escaping. Thick and brilliant red-clay
river-water, bloodying the ice.

Apple-green branches among the brown.
Stiff silk ovals pushing out of the tips of the uppermost.

I am in love with moisture.

Ambivalent about metaphor.

How transformation annihilates the source,

and motive conspires.

How *snow*

gathers in the blind eyes of statues, etc.

A man once loved a woman so much
he killed her,
so that he could know for sure

no other man could have her.

*

Yes, it's a metaphor:
a man once loved a woman so much . . .

Look, here's an emptiness, he said.

An emptiness of earthworms, even of
shellfish and of sponges . . .

Death.

No, that is not it. That is still not it.

You. Come closer. I want to tell you something:

*

Last night, my daughter saw a black kite
caught in the wires which run down Electric Avenue.

She thought it was a starfish,
stuck way up there without its mother—

without even a picture of its mother
it could look at and be comforted by.

      *

My neighbor says, *How come nobody talks about
the post-partum*

*depression? There's a
lot of women walking around out there*

*in Dante's kitchen.
Lots of them.*

      *

Samuel Beckett: *All the dead voices,*

They make a noise like wings,

Like leaves,

Like sand,

Like leaves.

      *

To think I didn't know what beauty was.

*

Sometimes I think I am the most motionless of women.

A poem for and against sonnets:

A breath of sea, the leaves of the peach tree are
now thick, green, quick as a pack of minnows
when the wind picks up, they turn and lean, deathless—

The rugged yucca sways beneath the weight of its
own new growth, O'Keeffe-like gray-green explosions
of leaves like knives, deeply shadowed, venereal—

I'm thinking of the woman in *Cries and Whispers*
thumb-pushing a piece of broken glass
into the soil of her body—cutting the

depth of the lie (that she loved him, that they were,
could it be, alive?) *Entice and destroy,* says the
yucca. Our lawn chair flaps by

like a Cubist chicken:
Be fruitful and hide.

*

How did you do it? It's the question
all new mothers ask: their own mothers
flown in from anywhere, holding,
for the first time, their daughters' trophies.

Unerringly. She winks at the infant.

Erratically. Like everyone else—
I did as well as I could. No better.

Why did you make it so hard—
my growing up—
my leaving? This, well, her
weak point as a mother—why
do I pursue it?

Fear of the mirror, she says, and holds
the baby's wobbly head, fontanel pulsing
like crazy, to her face.

Too neat, I say.

Fear of death. She puts my daughter on her belly,
wipes drool from her cheek with a cotton diaper.

You aren't afraid of death. I pick up the child.
She cries.

Mother takes her.

Tell me, I say.

She holds the baby over one arm (a true sister
of her generation—always underestimated—like
Plath, an admirer of Eliot
and Moore, Housman
and Dylan Thomas.). *When this one*

needs to tear herself from your side,
baby, you may

or may not survive the deathblows
of her caged-dragon fury—
the hissed-out
acids of her rage.

*

(Did you survive it?)

It's night. My daughter's
dream-wrecked in her blood red
crib—the one I bought thinking
it would cheer her. No.
The one I felt evoked
the carnage of birth. My mother
and I have champagne on the balcony.
A sedulous
orange tree; tall
distant palms; the hidden dance
of the planets. (What's that—
moon or ovum—behind the night's
blood draperies?) Between us
as always, the sense of
something pressing, something
withdrawn.

Did you survive it? I repeat,
having toasted the matrilineage.

But are you surviving?

(I write as if there were no sorrow like my sorrow.)

Yes and no.

I used to think they were lovers' quarrels,
The arguments I heard in the street here.

              *

Brush away
         the copper fur
                  of pine needles:

                  black soil; night.

Brush away the night: Earth's hide—

         shining,
                  moist (!), *illuminated,*

         skin of the gravely ill (the peach girl)
                  skin of a child.

              *

The nights we spent wringing washcloths—
ice cubes crammed yet unavailing in our metal bowl—
no matter what we did,
         we couldn't break or cool
the rhetoric of fever—

language of flashes and sighs, and teeth-jarring
                  trembling.

              *

Sunday. Year's end.

Something of citrus,
geranium, rain-dampened earth.

A fragrance, barely detectable,

unnamed, impalpable, somehow
caught and harbored in the sleeves
of my butterfly kimono.

A perfume
against ruin.
(Too beautiful!)

A zone of no
destruction.

NE ME QUITTE PAS

There are French
intellectuals
who say that a woman
kisses herself as she walks—
her legs
like two schoolchildren
whispering—

In the space
between stanzas,
which I will call
"the clearing"—
in "the clearing,"
in the most interior clearing—
something of herself
(the woman walking)
is disappearing—

is left standing at the station
in a vintage Chanel mini,
kissing another unreliable lover
adieu.

FROM SOR JUANA'S LAST DREAM

Be a child forever.

What my mother said
of her desire to see me
choose the cloistered life.
But I remember other
declarations—Mother and her
women friends agreeing:
There are women who have children
And women who are children.

What kind of sentence, then,
is the one she formed at the
beginning of my convent life—
a curse? Perhaps a fantasy
unspeakable in the company of
women, like herself, who had been
sentenced fertile.

FROM

POEMS FOR INFIDELS

TANGO OF FEAR

Let's   be clear   about the cow
in the trees   who stands
perfectly still   so that her bell won't
        make a sound.

    Her longing is
to be disobedient   so as to transform
and transcend what she is afraid of.

            How to make sense
out of   innocence, sorrow? How
to be not suspicious?
        We're only making
it worse for ourselves, staying home,
        crying over the missing bottles and
        blue ribbons.

Really,
little by little, fear wins. The cow is a mirror.
The trees dance in carnivorous revelry
        all around her.

TIGER-KITTEN

This creature always had you in mind.
You   in your cool phase like
early Antonioni   you
like an   old *milonga*   sobbing
about the slums   the purloined
lacerations of hard living. How
can pleasure taste so much like anger
        like grief? Who will find a cure
for the bordello virus?
                            This cat's
    inside you   syncopated to the
whiplash purr by purr. It knew you from
        the start. The zero of your soul.
The way you keep dredging up
obscene
cheap ironies. This dance is all about
                    truncation.
Don't forget   the tango master's
        verticality or   his verve.
Don't lose your nervousness. You
        feel a death-wish? Don't worry.
Let it escort you   into a haze of untamable
                    innocence.

DANCE OF RE-MEMBERMENT

Glance into a mirror: the poetic corpus.
          You are Laura
Scatterini, the goddess of dispersion, a
beautiful monster created out of every
individual perfection. Postponement is
          your thing. You lack parts.
You cry out to reverse it. A non-
Freudian way of looking at yourself seems
               urgent. But
    the libido returns, savage and non-
cultural, wearing long fringe and implants,
          waving its fetishes, dismantling
dogmatic packages, prescriptives.
Please the father/become the father/ah
          turn on him/talk to the trees.
    Make your nakedness a reason to
speak. See the present moment as an end.
          Your body as hope.
          Your body as word.
          Your body dancing alone
at the expense   of no one.
A tolerable   swirling
          nudity turning the
                         forbidden screws,
permitting a celebration in which   word
          turns back into flesh,   absence into
          heat, into light, into meaning.

ELEGY FROM A NIGHTINGALE'S POINT OF VIEW

Twit twit . . . jug jug . . . Tereu

He came as if in exile to a   docile
    West, having   long ago forgiven
his exes   who
     univocally seemed to be at
   their wits' ends when not
having   premonitions about him.

He   seemed   too
disorganized for the   Murphy bed
in the Peter   Pan   apartments on
    Second South where, at 47, he
   committed himself to   never
reaching   adulthood. Where he
fancied his   collections of fine pens and
   razors. Where on   occasion
he'd   artfully shave a woman's
   leg
then paint her biggest   toenail
   obsidian,   blowing on it till it
   was as hard as glass.   Then he'd
     measure out
a   coffee spoon of cocaine
powder over the   tip of it, and
    up   across the arch of her
foot, sometimes   trailing it off
   all the way to her knee cap.   You'd
  have to lie perfectly
still while   he scraped toward   your
    middle with his straw,
afterwards fastidiously
    licking with his king-
    of-cat's

tongue just those places where

                              the coke had been.

He wanted to be   like the man in the

          Magritte painting   whose

         head

was only sky—absolved of   all of it and

all-   absolving—

                   but maybe he wasn't able

to   forgive the   rapist of Philomel.

          And maybe behind the   fleshy

mask of his   face was the

                  smooth face of a

newer   mask. Maybe he

                did eat that much

speed. Maybe in   some book a

          picture of a train had

spoken to him, saying:

        Take me to the city built

        entirely of slaves of love,

and   so he'd taken it   (the picture)

somewhere, having   wanted to see for

          himself a city built by

      lovers or lunatics—   his twins.

Maybe   dying was

      a consequence of his

    rejecting certain   commonplaces

widely   proliferated in this time,

           the one perhaps which

claims a poet's life,

        well, matters . . . I

do think it was all

let go by him finally: the
girls with no tongues who
took his   poetry workshops, the
flies around the soda cans,
the song
96 *Tears* sung by that
LA punk band (as if
by a fly, the 96
tears coming out of its 96
multi-prismed eyes . . .),
the migrant workers'
banda music, the problem in
Utah of   getting a
martini dry. *I'll do*
anything for you,   he whimpered to
Bank of America in
the middle of the night once, pounding his
hand against an   impenetrable
drive-through window drawer until
he shattered a bone: *just let me have a*
little of my own money . . . If the
bank had been a
woman, it would've
given him what he
wanted. In
fact, a woman I
know came
forward with some
cash that night and
he left town with her,
looking from behind as if a
plump fetus were
pushing its head down through his
shirt collar, and I

never saw him again.   Maybe
        it was his
                tongue on my kneecap.
Maybe his baby-face,   or his
                rough beard or the
        wind coming in   freezing from
                the Uintas. Maybe the
way he assumed we'd all   been
                                forced to
                        do things that were,
in some other life, unthinkable, and
                        because of that, we were all both
        guilty   (of the knowledge)
and of the deeds,
whatever they were, and   also
                (just because, without
        a need for explanation)   just as
innocent as
                morning. Always starting with
        pure emptiness and
forgetting our   alibis. Some songs were
        prettier, he'd said,   *despite*

                the rudeness of our bringing them.
Maybe that was wisdom. Maybe it   was

        nothing but a kind of
                genius for seduction. At
        any rate, the time he
                dipped a razor edge
                        into a vein behind my
knee and
blood shot back,   staining his face, I

67

forgave him,   almost instantly—so
         difficult to see a person
      wreathed like that—
and starting to weep. Or laugh.   You know,
          there was no stopping it.

POEM

*(It's already the end of the month and I haven't
finished my essay on Larry Levis)*

My love affair with lilacs
uses up one more day at the desk.

A bush. The sprouting unerringly.

The dead face in the coffin   (his?   or that
gray-beard's?)   not more elegant
than my own. Don't
you feel them, all the ghostly undulations
here? More lilacs would purify this room.

Unhaunt it. Eros could slip out on Psyche,
leaving her satin flanks still damp. Her sex
still edgy . . .

The problem is that ghosts don't
evaporate. They linger in our caves; they

lick our ears. *We go without a trace,* is what
he keeps on trying to say to me.

The Story of O as Told by E

1.
Ever enter her eyes, Stephen?

2.
Ever seen her bed sheeted,
Ever seen her leg wrecked where she
Squeezes the Lethe-needles?

3.
Ever feed her? Ever yelled her pet letters?

4.
Ever get fermented, bent, metered?
Ever been deemed? Redeemed?

See, she never tells me, Stephen,
yet she seems demented, ethered.
She's egret-ended,
eel-edged. Let her be herself.

5.
Let me be selfless:
she needs gems. She needs eggs.
She needs cheese. Jeez,
Steve,   she needs her deed
reneged here!

6.

Bet she'll feel keen when they free her.

7.

Bet she'll even bleed new femme emblems.

CIRQUE DU LIZ AND DICK

Puerto Vallarta

Facing each other rather desperately—
his eye is like a star—
we stare and say, "Well, we have come this far."

She doesn't like the lizards, strewn
like dry white bones
all over everything.

Nor the way stiletto heels click
on the Saltillo tile that is
ubiquitous.

He drinks, and looks so bloody handsome.
Who dya think he'll make love to, Mrs. Burton—
Sue Lyons or Ava Gardner?

She feels discarded, fooling with her pearls
in the reptile torpor of the Mexican
Riviera. Key grips always

booming away somewhere beyond the patio.
He wants to be with her in London,
eating lemon pies. He longs for

the old delightful tracking down of
gloves to match a blouse or
just her drag queen whimsy.

Here it's all *la vida no vale nada.*
Life is worth nothing.
Part of her is sorry she became

"a public utility."
Part of him wants to do Hamlet again.
But he feels closer to Claudius,

marrying so quickly on top of the death
of the other marriage. A woman
is like glass, they say here:

always in danger.
Together,
they've renamed the town "Seething—"

They still have "that feeling of antenna—"
a quivering contact with each other.
Above her head she poses

another spray of artificial roses,
making him think of a novelty rodeo act
he saw a very long time ago in Wales.

AN ORNATE ENCOUNTER

In my guerilla youth, I worked as a nurse—
washing the angry bodies of the newly born one day,
combing the long, almost ephemeral hair of the not-yet dead
      the next.

What is the present?

A Chinese opera, billowing with red-gold silk. A stage
where all things are born simultaneously and simultaneously
bathed with history and future.

The place I walked earlier.

(Once again, Faustino, I'm dancing with you to the anachronisms
      of fandango.)

I don't know whether anything progresses. But it's here,
our baroque moment, gathering panache inside this ocean,
this plaza, this crevice in the sky's pale-blue acoustical shell:

librettos and chrysanthemums and eternity's slow-
opening.

FROM

BLUE SHADOW BEHIND EVERYTHING DAZZLING

A PORTAL ON THE FOREHEAD

It's so simple on a holy day to see with

the third eye—to recognize the cliffs and rivers

and white, winged horses of the vaster world.

Still, there are splinters in the brain

that vibrate

with a fierce nostalgia for the cloaked

life of blurred and disjointed vision—that ache

with love for the rough opacity of

things. One

wraps around the other—

so that on a rainy day in Sarnath a neem tree

might bleed pure mercury

out of its leaves, and flood us with

insight almost as if we recognized that particular

dance of alacrity and silver as something

we once did—and

will do again tomorrow, somewhere   deep within

the cicatrix   the hoof-wound

the yogi's   thumbprint the   marigold's aperture.

Go on, Sure, Why Not?

The gods walked along the path up the valley
like a caravan of ants.

My beloved black bamboo seems wrong

today   here   next to the live oak on my

terrace. Though as I say that I know it's

what I've said every time I've arrived at

this precise moment   before I pause then

notice a tribe of red ants stuck like dried

blood bits in thin cracks in the oak bark. To

go on   at that point   always seems an inadequate

description of   what it is we do when

Brahma wakes.   Even *living* fails to describe

this inhabiting of eternity in which we

pause occasionally and insist upon staking claim

to an aesthetic   point of view. *One wants*

to be singled out.   At the same time   one

wants to be hidden in a thicket of sharp

black leaves   to be nothing

but a pair of orange eyes   without

the human burden of self-awareness.   Pure fear

pure hunger   pure procreant urge   pure

thoughtless push.   When Hamlet says *My*

thoughts be bloody   *or be nothing worth*   he's

thinking too of the grave where there is

no thinking blood   no bloody thinking.

DOMESTIC ANIMALS

Who are these coming to the sacrifice?
To what green altar, O mysterious priest . . .

Make no mistake—   even the priest is

tethered to a pole and can   travel only as far

as his leash will   let him. The poem

can travel   only as far as the finger traversing

its field. I can go only as far as   age   despite

ceremony.   Face it   bold lover

we're piping ditties of   no tone—making

cruel disputes with enigmas over steak bones

our intertwining   monologues rising into an

ether of their own disintegration.   The only

option we've got is   to enter the coliseum the

studio lot   the sacrificial clearing with a   breezy

manner—to face the solemn   obtuse   intoxicated

or whatever gods   blissfully   disarming

in our ignorance   of how it ends.

SOMEONE GREETING YOU FROM AFAR

for D. B., RIP

Behind the barrier of daylight   a dark outline

you don't want to stare at for fear of being

blinded. It's the same   figure you recognize

in the pupils of enemies and lovers   consuming

itself in front of you   holding an unremitting

interchange with the clear universe of things

divine.   Everyone on the other side says

hi. Everyone says   the Beautiful is nothing but

the onset of Terror   we can barely Define. Who

is the Person greeting me behind the burning?

The thighs, the knees   emerge as black

silhouettes   against white. *Hi, hi!*   You know

it's too late to remain   Incognito. You don't know

whether or not   Death is kind.

WHEN THIS WARM SCRIBE MY HAND

goes cold

falls open (a last

gesture) congratulates

the sky   is finished with fluency

something

will shine in its palm   perhaps a

piece of the sun on her lotus throne

and there will be one

theatrical scrap of red

drapery somehow

hung there

(to demonstrate   how irresistible

both sacrifice and massacre

are?   Or

to mimic   a veil for a veil   that

illusory fire   without which

nothing in existence

          can give heat.)

What Is So Amazing

is not so much what is beneath

the house—   matter and dirt—

nor what is outside it—   surges of

light—   space that has no end—

but how it all seems   ever to

be renewed by something

un-erasable—   an energy

that drapes itself over everything

like   translucent film   so that

what was shabby   what was

perishable yesterday   today takes in

oxygen   makes an exchange

with the world   in that deep place

where   for lack of more clarity

I'll say matter becomes consciousness.

Those other questions   creation

death   free will   etc—

let's continue to defer   let them

simply be   unresolvable.   What's

so amazing is   this   apparently

unstoppable commerce—   that the

surfaces of all objects—   animate

inanimate—   and of all minds quaver

continuously like water—   reshaping

themselves into the same body—   the

world—   a candescent   breathing

being whose bright   exhalations are

a kind of compensation   for all of it.

FROM

SO QUICK BRIGHT THINGS

JADE NIGHT

Scenes of mad love. Days laid down
               like rags around their feet.
             Titania stands
with Oberon   looking at the ruin of ruins
           in Mexico.

   A fountain in the middle of the room:

     *

Nothing in the world   but rain.
Nothing in the world but rain and   rags and

their two beings rotating
                  totally washed. And
    this is the real place.   Rub it.

   Rub it till it tears you apart.

EFFUSION 1

Some of us
            are so obsessed with the lyric past
that we   die of it.

                        For some
it has the permanence of
            bronze   although it was conceived
in clay   or plaster.   Or by a
            bird
flirting   or murdering.

COUPLE WITH THEIR HEADS FULL OF CLOUDS

After their brush   with death
        but before either
    Titania or Oberon had spent any time
                        in Puck's yurt
    tripping their brains out   reliving
their births   this
        was the time they referred to as

"Clockwork and Despair—"

                    *

Statues were   in fact
        looking at them knowingly.
Seafoam   was made of gypsy   omens
        and cigar smoke.   But it was
what things were not   that made them
        difficult then.   What
        they were not   was magical.

What Scrapes the Clouds: a Digression, or Christopher Marlowe is Dead

After the funeral procession
                    the actors
        return once again
to the room. The poet-   killer
            is released from
custody and   joins them

a celebrated hero. What
                is a dead poet? A
metaphor for textual violence?

A type of
        censorship? A
                charm or trigger meant to
move them to a
        different level of discourse
altogether? The red
                    curve of
        his mouth had been
closed as if to refuse their kisses—

—And so they had buried him
a spent sun

at the nadir of all bottomless   reckoning.
Only   his
antlers remained—irregular
        structures stretched up into
                    darkness

the number of their branches
            corresponding precisely to the
        number of
        torments   he had borne.

TORTURED LITTLE SENSITIVITIES

Onto all of her sensations   she slips the handcuffs of a smile
knowing that with one   leap of her electric legs she could
initiate the   annihilation of Oberon. She sips
oolong tea in her fur-lined cup.   Checks her website
lifts the jewels on her arms   to see if the wounds they've
been covering have   festered or improved.

AFTERNOON OF A FAUN

How beautiful   his haunches.

How sleek his horns.

How awkwardly he   moves along
the dance floor

clicking in the direction of Titania
who's wearing a diaphanous caftan
                    and blue wings.

It's somebody's *quinceañera*—

                    *

fairy-babies in tiaras.   Girls
dressed like   Lady Baltimore cake.

A flamenco house band plays
                    Amor Milagroso.

But Titania has   done the math.
And simple vanity prevents her

from pursuing   her Nijinsky
like a pack of hunting dogs

into the woods   behind the
                    belle époque pavilion.

SPHINX-LIKE

The woman has been   self-othering lately.

Abandoning the   childlike   candor
    she'd cultivated for millennia. From now on it's
games of wisdom and clairvoyance—   not

the ingenuous fascinations   sparked by
chance meetings of   words   in a poem. She

still believes   of course   that the whole earth
                    is art—

and that the marvelous must be
integral to   everyday drama.

But she's stepped outside   the skin
of her former   muse/*femme enfant.*   She has

narrowed her gaze.   Her mane
                a mass of stone ringlets
                        trails down her back—a
monument to anarchy.

Not   failed anarchy exactly—

but to a rush and tumble
vivacity she no longer   seeks nor finds.

So many people die   anyway.

The future, a matter of staging—   more
staging—   more refusing to

conform   your words to your acts.

EFFUSION 5

after Magritte

The invisible pipe hides nothing.

Only the visible pipe, being seen,
remains in its mystery undiminished.

So it is with love. Of the visible love
one may say, "This is not
my love." Of the invisible love

one may say nothing. Otherwise
they are both pipes. Or
"pipes."

FROM
IMPERFECT PASTORALS

CLEARER THAN AMBER GLIDING OVER STONES

is the sunlight of thought. Quieter than the crisp fiction of windlessness—
production, consumption—

are you tired of convincing people you're not trying to convince them of
anything? I am.

Soil is necessary. Perhaps we could agree on that—
and stop cupping our hands beneath the sky as if it held what we wanted:

a name for what it is that happens in our minds when we're ecstatic and
          alone—
when

briefly destiny uncries, like someone in a movie weeping backward
(tears rolling upward from cheeks to eyes). Perhaps

nothing can outrun the rose of this mind-thriving, not even
the final, sealing hush of golden Buddha.

Maybe we're trapped innately, gnat-like, in the middle of great vacant signs.

Maybe we just think we are.

THE LIGHT AND SHADE UPON THE GLOBE

World or thought—which of the two thinks the other?

I think too much at the risk of seducing myself and

sashaying away through the topiary aviary of

life. What thinkst thou? That the earth is small

and blue, that doors and windows open onto ether and

death, that you'd go all the way to the moon and back

for a breakfast of Absolut and *fondue de poireaux.*

We're veiling our statues this morning so that whatever

music there is can be unabashed. We're garlanding an entrance

to the future—a portal—a mirrored tortoise shell. Now

we're thinking again! Thinking we can sustain the

whole planet with our moods. When only you can.

FOR NOT IN VAIN WE NAME THE CONSTELLATIONS

Distracted, I too wandered as far as the Pont Louis-Phillippe.
The winking of the stars I understood—metallic exceptions

and irritations, then the dawn of eyes and eyeing—of spilled
wine leaking into the mouth of the earth, or is it an ear

into which I can shout, scattering the names of my ancestors

all the way to wherever? Emptying temples, the day turning
this way, then that. Coffee with the poet who says, "I'm a fake.

A total fraud." Then dinner with the climatologist. I'm not
saying all of this is or isn't meaningful—it's just that I prefer

certain things to remain anonymous—unlike the bears circling
the illuminated Paris skyline. Or the swan soaring above its own

four-pointed reflection. Or the Seine weeping incoherently
but in French.

SO MUCH EFFECT HAS HABIT ON THE YOUNG

To each   her lair of solitude   the blur

and   spidery confines of being

(hovering personages   notwithstanding)

she wants engagement in the fungible aspects

of play   want to play with

some ur-word   a contingently configured

field of   potential on the page

(but oh my daughter there's nothing but water)

so she goes it solo   from the stony bottom

of the well   of solipsism   reading

as when we were children   and our

books broke   apart   in the infinite

breaking   of all words   and the hillsides

grew   crazy radiant   in confetti and

(the birds of the air filled her heart with despair)

WHAT DELAYS THE LONG NIGHTS

For cat ladies everywhere

Slumped au naturel in a rattan chair,
awash in the desert of my faithfulness . . .

Doors provide unexpected openings.
Windows, when not false, open "in

praise of the new polemic," producing
the desired effect of estrangement. Under

the circumstances, oppressed by desire, I
open a can of fish, if not worms, if not

dismembered mermaids; I kiss the bloom
of a captive orchid enigmatic as weeping

and as echo. Black cats move from room
to room. I remember the time my lover,

Aeolis, took on the raucous, rolling body
of an autumn storm . . .

DRY CRACKING SOUNDS ARE HEARD

The path ahead   glitters in dialectic.

Why do we feel instinctual—
     motley-clad?
                       It
     overwhelms logic.

We think answers
     can be found by pressing

against boundaries   yes so we press
          against beliefs, for

example, the philosophical given
that a thing   can only be true if it is

as beautiful as nature.
(Aristotle's reverence for natural beauty

was it based on
adoration or acquisition?   This is

something I'd
        like to know, as if
     the difference is more
        significant than the similarity
between

the two). Don't you love other people's
     shimmering
bits of thought—

walking through   words like a
        happy
and avaricious   zombie

clown—

(totally non-hierarchical)?

WILD BEASTS AND FISH, CATTLE AND COLORED BIRDS

I would not have lain in the grave of this body so long

were it not for the enticements of animal   life

were it not for tigers   (oh there aren't any left

you say   just skins and masks and inconsolable

shamans) were it not for   creatures   without

narcissism or fetishes.   Human desire is

avaricious.   Human desire   aspires on wings

says *gather it*   to symmetry   and form   and fear

but here we go again with spectator and voyeur.

Not wanting   to be either   I suppose   I would rather

cling   to a little long-haired   lamb with whom

curl by curl   I could enumerate the forests of the night

burning   more or less unremittingly.

ALONE, RATHER BECAUSE NOT OTHERWISE

I resemble   myself too much.   In that way I'm
ironic,   or allegorical.

There was the   time you   made a movie of me
I didn't know you were

making—somehow my   presence supposed your
absence, I suppose. So

I was once again   outnumbered. Still gently nursing the
wounds caused by caricature—

sucking the   last sweetness from   the illusion
of idiosyncrasy.   How did that

mouth kiss, I   wonder. How did that   ruined, magenta
hair beguile? In sepia, darling,

like all dream sex: solitude and object-hood a-bountiful.
Your head on the

pillow, fellow. And I,   Señorita Death.

THE HERON LEAVES HER HAUNTS IN THE MARSH

Let me go, domestic air, inner conflict and anarchism.
Let me replace

the thick veil of separation
with a thinner veil. The

anchoring point of a marriage is mythical. Catch me
off-guard and slip out for some whiskey

why don't you—

I'm not the one in the leather coat and the
comb-over makeover.

Over me the wind's dumb moan, beside
me the foam and glitter of the Pacific. The

heron has "one of the most begrudging avian takeoffs."

Oh fucking hell I'll go. Have I had a tetanus shot? Not
for years.

AND IN GREEN MEADOWS RAISE A MARBLE TEMPLE

The sound you hear it's a hammer chiseling time out of fragrance and our
pain it's a pas de deux of childhood dreams and generations' claims it's the

dance of a sand-grain in the stem-crook of a shoreline flame or it's you and
me pulling ourselves along an infinite chain of incongruities toward

unthinkable death (oh tissued scrim of history a skeleton man with a look
of pity asked me up to his apartment the best in New York City) that was long

before we fell into the ayahuasca lord lord and now that we've lost our talent
for impersonating lizards now that we've harvested for ourselves the long

green hair of a river now that we've pawned our ethnic jewelry from Cuzco
and Costco where's the poem that once once held it all for us all pleasure and

all sense and what is this over-intended sandwich of canned meat "boneless,
economical" oh monuments oh polychromatic Kali keeping beat

LIGHT CHAFF AND FALLING LEAVES
OR A PAIR OF FEATHERS

on the ground can spook a horse who won't flinch when faced
with a backhoe or a pack of Harleys. I call it "equine

optics" because it is a different kind of system—
not celestial, necessarily, but vision in which the small,

the wispy, the lightly lifted or stirring threads of existence
excite more fear than louder and larger bodies do. It's Matthew

who said that the light of the body is the eye, and that if
the eye is healthy the whole body will be full of light. Maybe

in this case "light" can also mean "lightness." With my eyes of
corrupted and corruptible flesh I'm afraid I see mostly darkness

by which I mean heaviness. How great is that darkness? Not
as great as the inner weightlessness of horses whose eyes perceive,

correctly I believe, the threat of annihilation in every wind-blown
dust mote of malignant life. All these years I've been watching

out warily in obvious places (in bars, in wars, in night cities and
nightmares, on furious seas). Yet what's been trying to destroy

me has lain hidden inside friendly-seeming breezes, behind
soft music, beneath the carpet of small things one can barely see.

The eye is also a lamp, says Matthew, a giver of light, bestower
of incandescent honey, which I will pour more cautiously

over the pathways I travel from now on. What's that whisper?
Just the delicate sweeping away of somebody's life.

DRAWN BY A TEAM OF THREE-LEGGED
FISH-TAILED HORSES

The road to death is crooked, even for a god. Your
three-legged fish-tailed horses never want to pull in the

same direction so the chariot lurches and jerks forward
in a confused motion, driving the charioteer to curse, to

use the whip, sometimes to crash against crusty underwater
cliffs or plummet into sudden drop-offs in the sea floor.

How much more difficult for poor humans caught between
the names of things and the iridescences of perceptions—

one minute walking alone and in love on a mountain path,
the next waking up on a clinic's cot face to face with

different pastures—out of this moment something suddenly
expressing itself in a poem, and out of that moment another

plummeting. Meanwhile herds of shapeless enormous seals
pasture in the sea above hidden flowerbeds. I live in a kind of

lurching and jerking amid shimmers, glimpses, and recognitions,
between the day and its passing. Last night I stood beneath

a coral tree whose black branches were full of snowy egrets
squawking and shifting before settling down for sleep. It was

a picture for a Roman tapestry! Almost an image for a poem!
And then I felt another plummeting. It had something to do

with beauty; something to do with the dogged willfulness of specificity and its opposite, all the alienated noncommittal

wavering of the sea. The beautiful sea. What could be more unbreakable?

DAYS SUCH AS THESE SHONE OUT AND WENT THEIR WAY

On the ploughed earth sits   an earth-brown person
wrapped in red and with a   tranquil expression devoting
herself to the taste and   consumption of a plant.

Roots are coming out of her shoes.   They grow out of
her clothing, on her wrists, the   folds of her sleeves, her
hips, and even the little box   lying on the ground next to

her has a thin blue root   cheekily stretching toward soil.
In this painting, which hangs   over the bar in one of my
favorite hotels in Oaxaca   the woman's belly seems to be

illuminated in the form of an   onion. Light-bulb/plant
bulb; when I'm lit as it were   I find this image hysterically
and stupidly germane.   A week ago I was drinking in a

different bar with a friend.   We ate mussels, and I imagined
us, Gail and Jaz, sprayed by   waves on a rocky breakwater—
these black and nacre shells   hunching in sunlight—far

far away from the calculations of   relationships and the cerebral
universe of signs. Above us   a painting depicted a chaotic,
bursting landscape in which   hands grew out of the ground

armed with knives. A floating   body, maybe Icarus, maybe
his sister, detonated into startling   flames. (Undoubtedly
these images have a   hidden rapport that would

require a lengthier conversation.)　　Marriages blow up
or last. Embryonic　　　　　　　　children become something
other than our　puppets.　　What's always tricky

is knowing when to read for　　　　　metaphor and when to
let the days shine out and go　　　their way.　On a road outside
my house, an indefatigable　　　automobile refuses to ignite.

Inside, a corridor leads　　　　to a great wooden staircase
upon which an amused nude　　　　lies in an almost Cubist sprawl.

LET NOT THE SPANGLED LIZARD'S SCALY BACK

distract you while you scale these boulders

or you'll miss the otherworldly doe and young
fawn picking their way through the ragged

archipelago of rocks toward Big Bear Lake with
its soft rim of marsh and burnt cedar not to

mention the moon hanging rather outrageously
low in the daytime sky I miss them

routinely because I'm watching a
bee war sometimes because I've been standing

in the funerary line of humanity too
long breathing solemn fog onto the face of

some humbling mirror none of this stops the
sky from continuing none of it explains the flashing

turbulence of serpent beside the path or
the bewildering shoal of blue wings above I wish

that my thoughts could be projected like light
thrown as if they were rays of light all over this

landscape would that constitute a reconciliation
or betrayal of all these differentiations

in all seriousness if I try to picture my thoughts
they look like souls in Botticelli's Hell like flames

some of them with buds of miniscule human faces
which is also what they look like in Paradise

IN THESE LATITUDES

   OF INDETERMINATE

      WAVES

                    —STÉPHANE MALLARMÉ

these oaks mark time in the tempo of centuries
one by my deck having taken twenty years to notice
I'd moved in next to it

every day with involuntary simultaneous
exhalations a brief exchange of our equally distinctive
aromas we say good morning before

going about our different yet proximate lives
bird-time is something more difficult to rhythm into
what with migration and wings

Wild Olives, Bitter-leaved, Alone Survive

Past the time of repast and the time of fasting
and the time of everyone going away, going back

to widowhood (yours the pang, but his the undiminished,
un-decaying gladness),

nothing to be done
but cart the suits off to Salvation Army, revise

the narrative—not what you had to say, always,
but a colder assessment: he never really had it in him

to be great. He was shady. Never thought things through
to the bottom, always half-grasping, sweeping by, ideas

spiraling up like ornate staircases into nowhere.
Should've died earlier. You say this to his shadow

arguing on your walks about who loved whom more fully,
whose happiness had depth, what has lasted.

Men "give their lives" they say, and women "give life"
and it all feels something like living inside someone else's

body, and then he dies and all that is ended, and
the usual remedy is to go and enter other lives (although

I just wrote "lies").

LET THOUGHT BECOME YOUR BEAUTIFUL LOVER

For then thought will be as noiseless as a mellowing pear, or it will lope out like a wind-wild unbridled horse, or pause with you on your balcony,

taking in the sea smell, not hearing the words of the poet saying love is an ornate piano, love is a seismic pulse; love is never anything a poet says it is.

It will be as enchanting as a wandering orphic singer in her little boat surrounded by attentive birds. Indeed, were I not now furling my sails and

hastening to turn my prow toward land, I might hold forth further on the topic. And you might think me beautiful.

WHAT NEED TO TELL OF AUTUMN'S STORMS AND STARS

It can hit you hard as a whip of grainy dust blown in
your eyes the realization that you need to tell someone

all of it even the worst in words not cheapened with showy
sound effects and with or without the dismembering con-

ventions of allegory—that you need to write about this woodpile
glowing between us like a dragon's hoard of gold-plated

bones—do more than to sit in the dust eating spiders and crust
whether or not you'll be taken for mad and if you are

taken for mad at least you'll be left alone. What can I tell you
about the evils of other people except that often I've found

human interaction to be a ferocious and almost feral feasting
not unlike the one Dante finds in which Count Ugolino

eternally feeds on the uncooked flesh of his son afterwards
wiping his mouth with the hair of the man he has just eaten.

Now that I've covered that let's step out into the autumn evening
and happily—perhaps drows'd with the fume of poppies—look up

because the dim lit sky is almost drooling with our dying
hence our wind-swept laments of gratitude and longing.

The bank all green with celery, the cucumber snaking

Thus I, too, come to the

world, Mrs. Dalloway (the world
in which trees drag their leaves
like nets through depths of air),

bearing flowers. And what of the
void? Today a hot wind of dust,
sandalwood, and musk is blowing

from the land of the dead. Moot
though it seems here in the idyllic
world, the emerald creek-side where

I epiphanize. In my own quaint way
I like living, I say, as my body, of its
own accord, pushes forth a parsimonious,

vegetal frill.

THE TREES THAT LIFT THEMSELVES SPONTANEOUSLY

The day's just handed me a glass-bulb pipe and an
energy drink despite my death-fetish. Now that

we've met, you can see I'm haunted by meaning and
both excited by and worried about the possibility that

writing is moving more deeply into graphic regions
such as actual figuration. I'm already quite aware

of the con game that is rhetoric but frankly I suck at
drawing, so how if that happens will I ever even start

to assert real authority in the life of my people? Oh
aleph-bet! And now the preverbal seagulls of San Pedro

cry by, above high-reaching greenery. I had nothing
to do with their rising, or with the trees meeting

united like lovers in the sky. The wind spins as quietly
as smoke here. I'm the woman filming it.

NEW POEMS

POETRY

Whether it comes nude and ardent to you,
Or whether it beckons out of faraway cypresses;

Whether it be astute or swallowed up in your endangerment,
Embedded in your window's sheen, an imperceptible enigma,

You, parting the clouds with imagination's keenly lit tentacles,
Can graze the inalienable formalities of its murmur.

I can see plain day and its masters making the reaping machinery
Of purgatory glisten in the deepest star-fires of your eyes.

By all means, be beguiled by this. And then I'll describe
The agitation in my labyrinth—how exquisite it has been—

To lift from a wayside altar poetry's quickening string—
How like being in love: the injury cringing in the mirror

Vanishes as you pass it, loaded down with death, leaving
Behind only a dazzling gust of panic and happiness.

Let's Not Fetishize the Negativity

We weren't watching the waves as they crested, tumbling toward us. That they reiterated canyons, sinking down between high points, we knew without looking. The weather wasn't a storm denying its destiny but an ephemeral tyrant whose song and custom we adopted. It didn't keep us angry or evoke the overwhelming idioms of the imagination. What non-interference could have freed us? Nightly wildness had come; sweat embraced it before succumbing to its chill. Addicted to disclosure, addicted to visibility, we were failures that would one day pack it in. Knowing this was a kind of victory.

THE ONLY THING WE HAVE TO LOSE IS LOSS ITSELF

Take from yourself what is always absent in you.

You won't misinterpret the spring rain overflowing the gutter and splashing
    on the bricks.

Take from yourself the pool of it, and the sorrowing, the mouths on people's
    faces.

You won't treasure these disappearances until the death-phone rings again;

For everything is ash-choked, delighting in catastrophe;

And for the person who can foresee the planet's foregone end,

Nothingness is of no use. In my world, not even the poem rising from mud,

Rebellious and alone, loses its losses. I won't let it.

BRUSHING AGAINST THE THERE

Beyond leaf-drenched waking—
where our high hills swell, foggy, in spite of the drought—

This is where I sweep the shrill remnants of
late morning into day
after pedaling beside

there where the road drops off dangerously—

where one day
before our dropped jaws and stammering
a nexus of various exiles congealed

cruelly inserting
its sentences into memory,
like a petty-mouthed child acting up among us.

This much
we are certain of—
what a furrowed and turbulent world

we shy from, once again—it blows, it blows
in meaningless noise
on imagination's most aromatic horizons—

the shapely yet impenetrable curtains
of History
opening briefly between us and
the there
where our lives will diminish.

Now though, the heretical sea,
our friend, rushes in and we too
heighten and brighten,

soul-crossed,
the ever-pearly membranes of our privacies intact.

PHOTOGRAPH

A photograph of me—I who am old, reader, like you will one day be—
No beauty.
And no one plucks the most pluckable yellow grapefruit suspended behind me,
Not you, suspended, I hope, in a moment of generosity.

And whatever else is nearby, flame-fed by a hummingbird's irradiated flicker,
Entered the frame without my noticing,

And left as soon as the blood-shutter carried out its tick.

I am envious of its disappearance,
Desiring as it did neither your attention nor your patience.

But we're getting along famously now.

You, both inveterate selfie-taker and neo-formalist,
Trying to decide whether or not this portrait will be up to snuff—
Me, for whom the question is irrelevant, for whom it was too late many lifetimes
    ago.

THE PETTY INFINITE

The jasmine by my studio is flowering—
Oh simple life on the surface of the planet.
My writing limbo oscillates before it.

Then the other plants begin to waken
And the ground perks up.

I am a madwoman, living
In the midst of such profound activity—
And such smallness.

Let love take its chances here.
Let love luminesce and mark time
In this yellow mill-wheel of days.

We existed here
Where the owl swayed on top of the
Swaying cypress tree.

What did we want from each other?
To die having said it all—
To win having lost it all—

One fragile about-face from the stars.

Yes, shorter is the crooked path and darkening doorstep of the person who has found me here. Who, awake and ahead, causes my peacefulness to arise. Road upon road, if he departs, it is to appear again somewhere transcendentally.

Sometimes his hands graze mine, yielding only a clover flower spark. That night which shortened the misery between him and me is now not locatable. Every part of the past is suddenly unavailable. And yet this existence, expressed, remains in everything loose, full, outside of us, where our separate destinies, scattered, are no more obedient than deer hunters' arrows, which scatter in the yellow field.

We are, as we dream ourselves to be, something green in a flash, the vertical torch of a cypress tree. We hover in the hills like a layer of fog, the azure sleeves of our spa robes unfurling.

(Of course, I mean that last image to be amusing, self-critical, and still somehow germane. Why not want everything?)

HOUSE WITH TWO WOUNDS

You and I shrink back into moralities we've invented,
always belittling them to diversion.

The freedoms of our failures lead us away from more august imaginings.

We live with each other as with two visiting immortals.

Friend, where has our beguilement gone?

My feet worn out by running excitedly among the ethers, let our dreams divide
us from ourselves with all their glassy fury.

Beeswax moon, remain tangled in the oak tree.

The mind harms us only when we're weak.

We let the house itself decide whether or not to collapse around us.

Conspiratorial We

Hammers and fingernails withheld
Even in the midst of frenzied days and envies

Nonplussed sun which moves behind mountains to
Caution the edges of our eyes

Mouths which nothing can out-die
Under the disordered dusk, through mysterious windows

We meet and conspire, bathe our daydreams in gin
So much said already in the twilight

We are alive, but do not demand much of it
We don't believe in anything but ghosts

We don't question people badly dressed in mourning
Under the heavy heel, we are alive and weightless

Under the capsized boat we fly

A Mountain of Pins

Our little house is built
On a mountain of pins.

A *camino real* stops at our door.

Around it, life awaiting;
Constellations.

Inside it, you
With your scar measuring
Abilities and
Bird-down eyelashes.

AGING

We have not acclimated ourselves to the changes.

Had we been articulate like the plants and prayerful to the moon, paying close attention to its scars wound with jasmine, had we been simple like the black sea glittering, in love with its seabirds, had we not lived until winter, had the sky shuttered its thin blue eyelids, had our thinking atoned for us.

Look, planet fields, tombs, our oneness. The cough of thunder reiterates the jerking progress of what is inevitable. On the threshold of death, only our dreams' perseverance maintains its ongoing arguments with memory, with gardens, with the now-or-never everything of these vestigial days.

THE AVOCADO TREE'S REBIRTH

A mockingbird surveys the living room. I dream the butterflied leaves asleep. Let the tender-eyed sky whose air I breathe efface the terrace where I write.

The height of the born again tree renews my reverie. How still it is, this cave of green, cave of the purified wind admired.

I know that a fiery creek-bed will be my undoing. That, and the lie of a harp my art requires. And the words, the words, the soil, the hollow billowing of hope that is hoisted like a pirate's flag above this enchanted shipwreck.

JASMINE

I witness the masked towhee that, daunted by springtime's robust sky, steadies itself in the embalming vines of the white-starred evening's greenery.

No longer drug-induced, just sane everyday tiredness. No more writerly
         depression. Only
the wind in the pass whose cool breath is everywhere among my mind-drifts.

I disavow the horrors of nightmares at the joint-roller's request.

On my laptop a gazillion fears weigh less than an eyelash.

The thin lines of the unknown curl and uncurl right in front of me.

Their clarity exhausts me.

HISTORIANS OF THE DEFEAT

I'd rather compose romances for you.
—Vladimir Mayakovsky

There is a malady here. It sparkles in a kind of haziness, has a homespun fragrance, arranges its facets in a pleasant enough manner. But come the victory celebrations, how devastating for those of us in the opposition. What a hurry up to a heartbreaking end.

For some, the defeat was death in disguise. For others it was simply stolen life.

There is no bottom to this defeat, no ceiling. At the end of all of our detours it is there, stewing in its domination, shining in the spittle it drops onto our fathers' disorderly tombstones.

Our poets utter laments, remember the times they envisioned the silhouettes of soaring birds, or of beautiful women, the times that waterfalls offered epiphanies. Some wish to remain unknown, cut off from their resources, to wait for the censorship that is coming.

Lovers lie in their beds alone, in naked exasperation, having brought to this moment nothing but subterfuge and vanity.

Automatons or innocents, the ones who build these walls, these blockades.

Even the planet we were born on is pessimistic.

I bind myself to a dying palm tree. In this position at least I am ungovernable.

TONY

In the urn of the lengthening day
The man who will die on my street
Is walking backward toward traffic

With his shirt on backward,
A bright orange vest, backward, and
His dirty white hair straight up

As if it were fire.
The rush of a sunset briefly
Appeases him by making windows vivid.

Then a dusk of gray lilacs.
An acrobatic bend of hillside
Seems to prolong the impossibility

Of his salvation. Though
Beleaguered, his brain is stuck on
Hope. (*My girlfriend,*

The German film-maker, is pregnant—
With twins! he says, dangling two used
Baby shoes in front of me.) He sings

A rough-hewn lullaby.
Virginia, his sister, whispers
Zen prayers in a single whimper.

She helps him sit down in front of the café,
More helpless than a bird, she thinks. But he is
Grinning, thanking God for the kindness

Of the yellow-haired goddesses who
Drive by waving. *Hey, Tony,* they say
How's life in the fast lane?

It's a fucking nightmare, he replies.

HOW IT'S DONE

My one daily cigarette entertained by its poisons, my heart's mind
Seduced by windows and wooden masks

May the one who lives in the room of transformations, awaking,
Summon some Spanish darkness

In poetry there is still the great still point, that primal piccolo whistle of death

Early in the day I sit to eat of the losses I need for my strength
They taste dusky, like honey, like medjool dates from the Mojave

Nightmarish kisses shaped by dread flash and retreat away
Only the clash of bamboo and wind lingers, reassuringly

When at last I open my keyboard to a winking whiteness, all the recesses
Of vowels collapse, fall flat at the glass feet of millennia

In this state, a black horse, towering, arrives, offers me his back
I decline, preferring to cross this particular river alone

He pushes the crumpled water up ahead

I write the names of sexual organs on my screen
They preen themselves and wink back at me

Keep Me Violent, She Says

I answered riddles
Drank poison
All around me buildings kept enlarging themselves

I felt the monumental height of the law

But death avoided me
Danger

Which will never be destroyed by this world
Mad for prisons

Took from me all melancholy

Took me back to the start of the old strength debate

A lie detector's needle spelling out my fear
And my resistance

THE POEM RINGS TWICE

Still, there's a crooked footprint and a dark sidewalk where Love had left me. Where, conscious and unbound, did it go? Perhaps it can be found in the blue algae of the river shallows.

Sometimes Love pressed against me, yielding only an enigmatic argument. Sometimes it watched as I stacked bracelet upon bracelet on my arms.

I sleep in its absence, not suspecting that I carry in my dreams the blade of life ever after.

Other mysteries remain—fluid, full, inessentially outside me, where my narratives, reimagined, are no thicker than glass pipe stems.

Alone in the shadows, I have stopped speaking. When I question the guessing, the wait, an aching begins. It moves from palm frond to street sign,

which the detective, this time, will not interrogate.

PERILOUS OBSERVATIONS

Tongues are in the gutters, branches like tongues hang from the trees. So licked, the night goes to sleep, cherished in the dark.

The days of not drinking and the days of drinking, one following the other in a rash of scrappy light, have made an alliance. They pass by together. They embrace.

Our intrusions are ant-like, given the glad thresholds in the mind, the gaudy future, the perfume, like a kind of armor, around the lemon tree.

River on the path, you are unresponsive to the fisherman but garrulous to the lost like me. Who's to know, under the swoons of time, if the mouth, rhymer of our needs, should not foretell but swallow?

If, as they say, resentments, unresolved, simmer like a stew whose flavor grows richer, years ago I could've eaten mine with a shovel.

Let's face the facts, humanity has blown it.

DRIVEN INTO NOWHERE BY THIS POEM

Come on, sterilize it,
Too, your comedy-
Charged, three-
Footed, limbic imagination,

So that its rhythm, milky and
Distant, ocean-
Filled, where
Cowardice borders on congratulations,
Congratulations on cowardice as well,
Brightens,

So that it
Re-elects the ninny
In the mirror, who
Processes mouth-shapes
For the half-starved ears
Of actors.

Pull it up on land
By its sea-drenched hair,
Hitchcock blonde, roots
As black as the those
Of the
Immediately electrocuted
Tree.

THE NON-SELF

Sewn through by my use
Of dashes,

Articulate
In the tongue-swallows of my
Clamped down mouth,

Clamped down
On this eyelid-thin
Life of mine. She is
Promiscuous—
A social butterfly. She

Wakes wearing
Spider-fern
Antennae and
Sun's motes,

Her
Fingers suggestively
Exploring a conch shell's
Cavity.

Or is it my hand that
Strokes and probes
The chalky interior
Of this metaphor?

YOU GAVE ME A NECKLACE

elegy for Claire Kageyama-Ramakrishnan

Like Vishnu, you wrote, *you are always with me.*
Gods are such a pain in the ass! I wrote back.

Later on, I'll ask you to tell me about the moment you know—
the moment that cannot be known.

Now, though, watching shadows grow on the side of this somber mountain,
just delirium and grief.

That, and the water's continuous erasing.

.

BRETON IN MEXICO

after meeting Frida Kahlo

Beside the cobalt blue of your wall he'd give you a kiss—a simple respite, oh marvel, from painters' soliloquies—if you didn't find him ridiculous.

In Coyoacán he'd write to you of *passion hiding its amethyst teeth in the black* . . .

He'd show you the keyless door to his psyche's dungeons, dance with you in slippers lined with jaguar fur, drink mezcal with the exiled Trotskys of Russia, Leon and Natalia Sedova.

For you, Frida, he'd be a tourist of dusk, a tourist of pyramids, of bodegas, of pain. Instead he's just a man waving goodbye to a window, to a particular color of blue, to Jacqueline Lamba, to Surrealism.

THE FINAL LAVA

The weight of the grape puts a hold on the tragedy of the afternoon.

Yet the glories of youth are a world-joke. Broke and symbolic, the wild-haired walker who cried to the river, carrying with her into history's prehistoric night a taboo rosary, arrived for the late shift at her kitchen job.

Her hopes were grave and remote. She blackened her eyes like Nefertiti. She dreamed: a mountain dripping endlessly wet with the fiery saliva of an epoch. She pawned all of her jewelry for a drug dealer's lawyer.

On the screen of my watchfulness, far from the diffusing mirrors of moon and sun, the daily world of imprisonment, of networking, of deportation, of torture and wildfire takes on the shape of a pyramid and threatens to spew something it will no doubt soon regret.

(We won't just get blasted to smithereens; we will watch ourselves get blasted to smithereens.)

The woman I used to be wonders: where are anyone's apologies for any of this?

MOTHER'S DAY

I left for a long time. When I returned, I'd invented a speech and spoke its tenderness under the petal-laden swaying of nascent summer. What did you whisper, Mother? Where have you hidden, Child? Then came an evening when her speech no longer recognized itself in its metaphors of divinity. When the sun's copper turning the surface of the ocean fuchsia simply hurt me.

AN AUTOBIOGRAPHY

Scrambling through weathered and frenetic academies, escaping from infrequent inspiration, armed-to-the-teeth dreams, domestic omens of infertility, brain-racked at the lips of cups, memories that can't be conjured. Mountain-top cabin, in your frog-rich mud, a bright delight once gave birth to a capsule of happiness.

Love left to another's mercy, what did I write of—infrared houses haunted by pasts, by families bitten with insanity? Something I wanted to be known. My fury appeased. What had hollowed out my belly, anesthetized my heart, perverted my scheming. Funeral flowers, removed from the tomb of the un-known listener, I buried with a simple wave. All this I wanted to be blinding and perceived.

Author's Notes

Twenty-three: The first two lines of the poem are taken from Petrarch's 23rd canzone in *The Rime Sparse,* translated by Robert M. Durling. The title also refers to the age I was when I wrote the poem.

She & I: The writing of this poem was inspired by the book *The Oval Lady* by Leonora Carrington.

III: Thinking about Rene Magritte

VII: "Reasonography" is a word invented by Chuck Rosenthal.

The Other: a pseudo-villanelle

The Main Attraction: The epigraph is taken from Cleanth Brooks' *The Well-Wrought Urn.*

Ceci n'est pas un morçeau de fromage: More thinking about Rene Magritte

The Ultimate Unknowability of Women: This phrase is taken from a jacket blurb describing one of the themes of Harold Pinter's work.

A Curse is meant, in part, to be a response to James Wright's poem "A Blessing."

The Earth as Desdemona: "Unerringly" is a Walt Whitman word; "Let us talk of graves" is from Shakespeare's *Richard II;* "The man" in the line "the man had no pity" is Ted Bundy; the image of snow gathering "in the blind eyes of statues" is a Larry Levis image; the Beckett quote is from *Waiting for Godot;* in the section "A poem for and against sonnets," *Cries and Whispers* refers to the Bergman film of that name.

Ne Me Quitte Pas: (Don't leave me) refers to the Nina Simone song, but in this case the plea is addressed to the speaker herself.

Sor Juana's Last Dream: A small section from "Sor Juana's Last Dream" which takes as its model, loosely, Sor Juana Inés de la Cruz's *"Primero Sueño"* (First

Dream), a visionary poem written sometime around 1685.

Elegy from a Nightingale's Point of View: An elegy for the poet Larry Levis. The epigraph is taken from T. S. Eliot's "The Waste Land." The last line of the poem refers to the Sylvia Plath lines "the blood jet is poetry/there is no stopping it" from her poem "Kindness."

Poem: The italicized line is a line of poetry by Larry Levis.

The Story of O as Told by E: This poem refers to *The Story of O,* by Pauline Réage and is an OuLiPo poem.

Cirque du Liz and Dick: This poem alludes to and quotes from the Elizabeth Bishop poem "Cirque d'Hiver."

The poems in the book *Blue Shadow Behind Everything Dazzling* were written in India.

Go on, Sure, Why Not?: The epigraph is taken from Hindu legend. The italicized line is Mark Jarman's.

Domestic Animals: The quoted lines are from "Ode on a Grecian Urn" by John Keats.

So Quick Bright Things: Characters in this sequence of poems are based loosely on characters in Shakespeare's *A Midsummer Night's Dream.*

"*Clockwork and Despair*" is an allusion to the work of Marcel Duchamp.

Imperfect Pastorals: The titles of most of the poems in this book are taken directly from *The Georgics,* by Virgil, L. P. Wilkinson translator.

Wild beasts and fish, cattle and colored birds contains references to William Blake's "The Tyger" and to the philosophy of Jean Baudrillard.

The god in *Drawn by a team of three-legged fish-tailed horses* is Neptune.

Days such as these shone out and went their way: The epigraph is taken from Alain Robbe-Grillet's *For a New Novel: Essays in Fiction.* "Jaz" is Jazmin Aminian Ventura.

The bank all green with celery, the cucumber snaking refers to the main character in the novel *Mrs. Dalloway* by Virginia Woolf.

Historians of the Defeat was written after the 2016 Presidential election in the U.S. The Mayakovsky quote is taken from "At the Top of my Voice."

How It's Done: One line taken from Robert Frost's poem "The Most of It."

Breton in Mexico: The italicized line is André Breton's.

Acknowledgments

Poems in this book have appeared in the following journals and anthologies, some in earlier incarnations:

88: A Journal of Contemporary Poetry; A Poetry Congeries; Antioch Review; Blackbird; Boston Review; Calyx: A Journal of Women and the Arts; Catamaran; Chicago Quarterly Review; Circulo de Poesía; Coiled Serpent; Crazyhorse; Cutthroat: A Journal of the Arts; Denver Quarterly; The Drunken Boat; Grand Passion: The Poetry of Los Angeles and Beyond; Gulf Coast; Hunger Mountain; Hurricane Alice; identitytheory.com; Laurel Review; Lips; Locuspoint; The Offending Adam; Pistola; The Poet's Child: Poetry; Poetry International; Pool; Pratik; Prime Number Review; Quarterly West; The Quarterly; Runes; Santa Monica Review; Spillway; Substance; Teesta Rangit (India)*; Third Coast; Verse Daily; Virginia Quarterly Review; Volt; Wide Awake: The Poetry of Los Angeles and Beyond; Yew Journal; Zócalo Public Square.* I would like to thank the editors of these journals, as well as the editors of the presses which have published my books: New Poets Series (Clarinda Raymond), Copper Canyon Press (Michael Wiegers), Red Hen Press (Kate Gale), Hollyridge Press (Ian Randall Williams), and What Books Press (Glass Table Collective, especially Kate Haake, Rod Val Moore, and Mona Houghton). Thanks as well to Robbin Crabtree, Dean of Bellarmine College of Liberal Arts, Loyola Marymount University, for a grant that supported the publication of this book.

I would also like to thank Diane Seuss for the insanely fabulous few years that changed my life, my poetry, *and* my eye makeup; my poet-comrades Molly Bendall, Karen Kevorkian, and Alicia Partnoy who have kept me alive and writing over the years; Marlena Dalí and Skye Gellmann who never fail to inspire and delight me; my champion and a constant source of inspiration David St. John; my good friends far and near, Antonio Leiva, Mary Mammarella and Tony DeAnnuntis, Daniel Tiffany, Theresia deVroom, Michael Ventura, Jazmin Aminian Ventura, Richard Katrovas, Virginia Morris, Elena Karina Byrne, Judith Taylor, Sarah Maclay, Holaday Mason, Ramón García, and Aaron Blackburn; my brother Bill Freimuth and sis-in-law Christi Engel for abiding friendship and inspiration; my brother Kurt Freimuth and sis-in-law Debi Freimuth for their consistent encouragement and love; my Tebot Bach workshop for keeping me on my toes; my Beyond Baroque buddies, especially Laurel Ann Bogen; Dennis Maloney for responding to my work with alacrity and insight; Elaine LaMattina for her beautiful book design; and finally, Chuck Rosenthal (aka Shark) for his sustaining love, his humor, his insatiable intellectual curiosity.

THE AUTHOR

Gail Wronsky is the author, coauthor, or translator of fourteen full-length books of poetry and prose. Her titles include the poetry collections *Dying for Beauty* (Copper Canyon Press), finalist for the Western Arts Federation Poetry Prize; *Poems for Infidels* (Red Hen Press); *Bling & Fringe* (coauthored with Molly Bendall, What Books Press); *Fuegos Florales/Flowering Fires* (a translation of Argentinean poet Alicia Partnoy's poems, Settlement House Press), winner of the American Poetry Prize; and *Tomorrow You'll Be One of Us* (Dadaist sci-fi poems, What Books Press), coauthored with Chuck Rosenthal and illustrated by the Los Angeles artist Gronk. Wronsky's poems and translations have appeared in many journals, including *Antioch Review, Boston Review, Poetry, Lana Turner, Guesthouse,* and *Volt.* The recipient of an Artists Fellowship from the California Arts Council, she is currently working on another art/poetry collaboration with Gronk. She lives in Topanga, California, and teaches creative writing and women's literature at Loyola Marymount University, where she was awarded the Harry M. Daum Professorship.

Author photo: Ty Cole